# Violin Duet Time

## 1 Minuet

Domenico Zipoli
(1688–1726)

# 2 Intermezzo

*(from 'A Midsummer Night's Dream')*

Felix Mendelssohn
(1809–1847)

# 3 Entr'acte from 'Rosamunde'

Franz Schubert
(1797–1828)

# 4 Sextet: Chi mi frena

*(from 'Lucia di Lammermoor')*

Gaetano Donizetti
(1797–1848)

6

# 5 Das klinget so herrlich
*(from 'The Magic Flute')*

W.A. Mozart
(1756–1791)

# 6 Grass, O green flower

Bulgarian

# 7 Tyrolean

*(from 'Guillaume Tell')*

G. Rossini
(1792–1868)

# 8 Ein Mädchen oder Weibchen

*(from 'The Magic Flute')*

W.A. Mozart
(1756–1791)

*Also Mendelssohn*

*Transfer to viola*

# 9 La Calumnia
*(from 'The Barber of Seville')*

G. Rossini
(1792–1868)

14

# 10 Folk Dance from the Canary Islands

Trad.

# CHART PLAYLIST

© 2007 by Faber Music Ltd
First published by Faber Music Ltd in 2007
3 Queen Square, London WC1N 3AU

Arranged & Engraved by Camden Music
Edited by Lucy Holliday

Designed by Lydia Merrills-Ashcroft
Photograph from Redferns Music Picture Library

Printed in England by Caligraving Ltd
All rights reserved

The text paper used in this publication is a virgin fibre product that is manufactured in the UK to ISO 14001 standards. The wood fibre used is only sourced from managed forests using sustainable forestry principles. This paper is 100% recyclable

ISBN10: 0-571-52932-1
EAN13: 978-0-571-52932-2

To buy Faber Music publications or to find out about the full range of titles available, please contact your local music retailer or Faber Music sales enquiries:

Faber Music Ltd, Burnt Mill, Elizabeth Way, Harlow, CM20 2HX England
Tel: +44(0)1279 82 89 82 Fax: +44(0)1279 82 89 83
sales@fabermusic.com fabermusic.com

# FEBRUARY SONG

## Words and Music by Marius De Vries, Josh Groban and John Ondrasik

1. Where has that old friend gone, lost in a Feb-ru-a-ry song?
2. Where is that sim-ple day, be-fore col-ours broke in-to shades?

— Tell him it won't be long 'til he o-pens his eyes.
And how did I ev-er fade in-to this life?

try to get a-way from this cra - zy world

6

# HOW TO SAVE A LIFE

**Words and Music by Joseph King and Isaac Slade**

1. Step one,___ you say___ we need___ to talk.___ He walks,___ you say,___ "Sit down,___ it's just___ a talk." He smiles po- lite- ly back at you. You stare po- lite- ly right on through

# LIFE IS BEAUTIFUL

**Words and Music by John McDaid, Simon Walker,
Bruce Gainsford, Bryan McLellan and Garrett Lee**

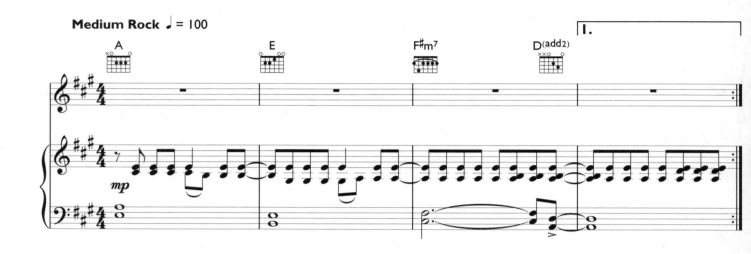

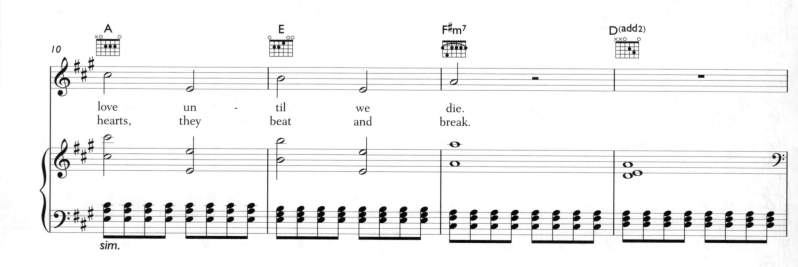

# LITTLEST THINGS

**Words and Music by Lily Allen, Mark Ronson, Santi White, Pierre Bachelet and Herve Roy**

# OPEN YOUR EYES

**Words and Music by Gary Lightbody, Nathan Connolly,
Jonathan Quinn, Paul Wilson and Tom Simpson**

Tell me___ that you'll op - en your eyes,___

tell___ me___ that you'll op - - en your eyes,___

tell___ me___ that you'll op - - en your eyes,___

tell___ me___ that you'll op - - en your eyes.___

# SHE'S MY MAN

## Words and Music by Scott Hoffman and Jason Sellards

♩ = 180 **Brightly with swung quavers**

(Guitar)

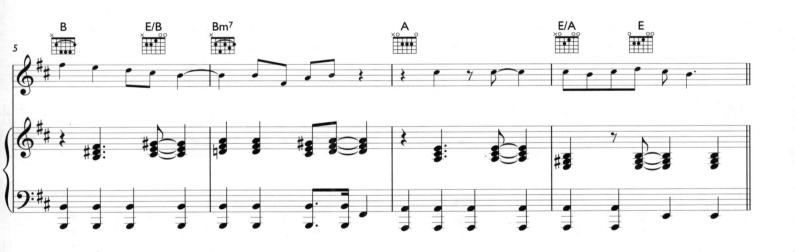

# PATIENCE

**Words and Music by Gary Barlow, Jason Orange,
Howard Donald, Mark Owen and John Shanks**

Moderate pop ballad ♩ = 90

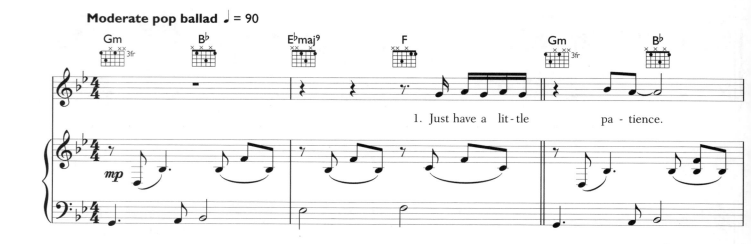

1. Just have a lit-tle pa - tience.

I'm still hurt-ing from a love___ I lost___ I'm feel-ing your frust-

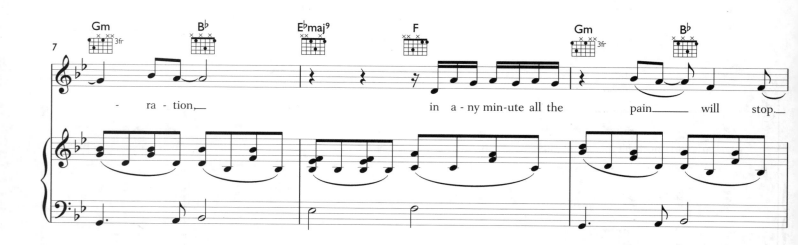

-ra - tion,___ in a - ny min-ute all the pain___ will stop.___

# ROSÉ

**Words and Music by Dan Gillespie Sells and The Feeling**

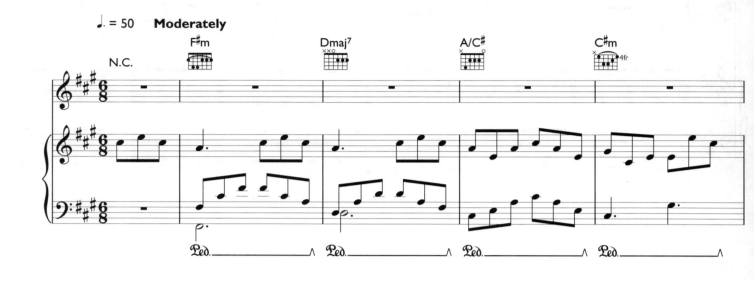

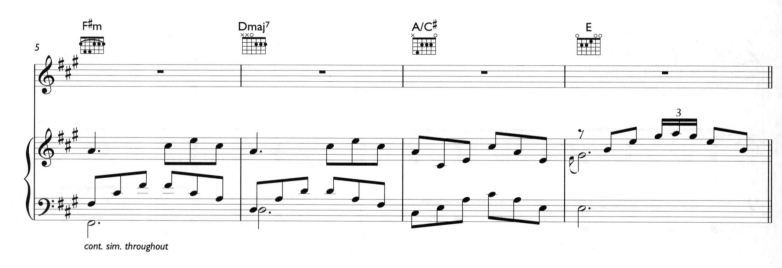

cont. sim. throughout

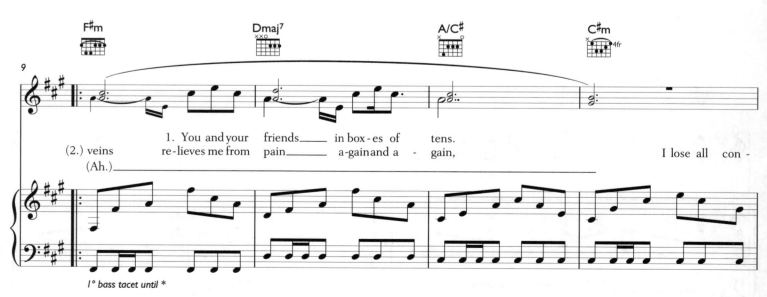

1. You and your friends in box-es of tens.

(2.) veins re-lieves me from pain a-gain and a - gain, I lose all con -

(Ah.)

1° bass tacet until *

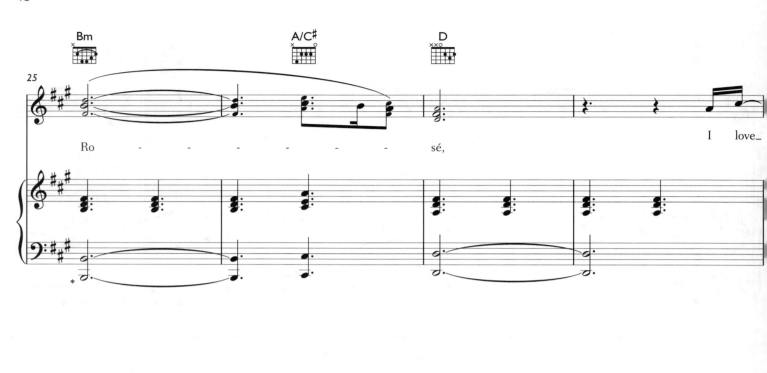

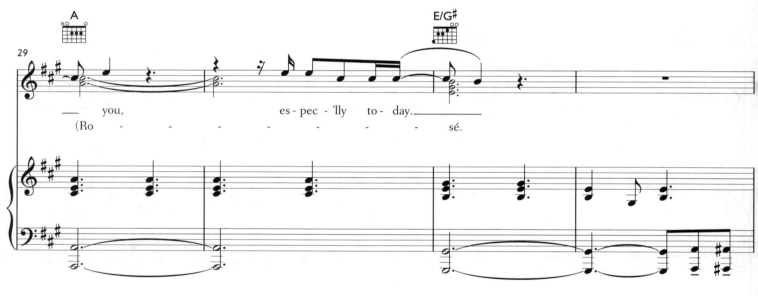

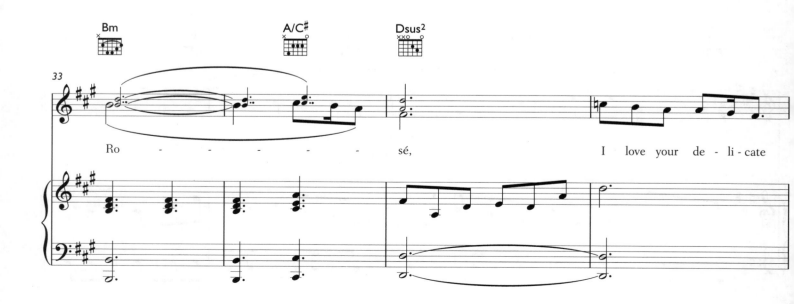

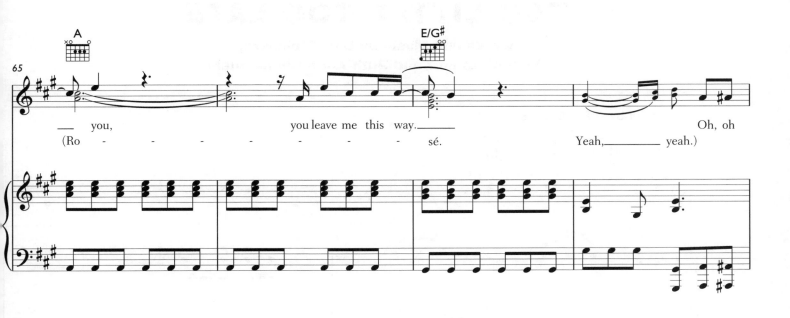

— you,                you leave me this way.____                                    Oh, oh
(Ro - - - - - - - sé.                    Yeah,_____ yeah.)

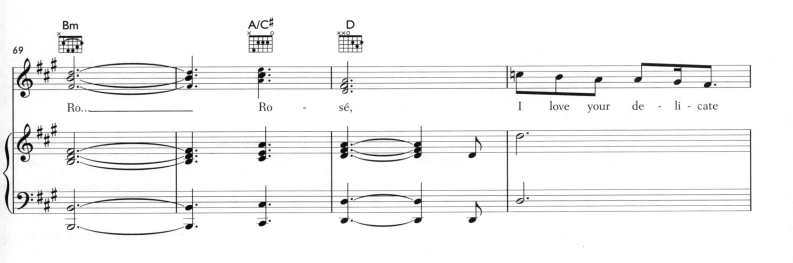

Ro.._____ Ro - sé,        I love your de - li - cate

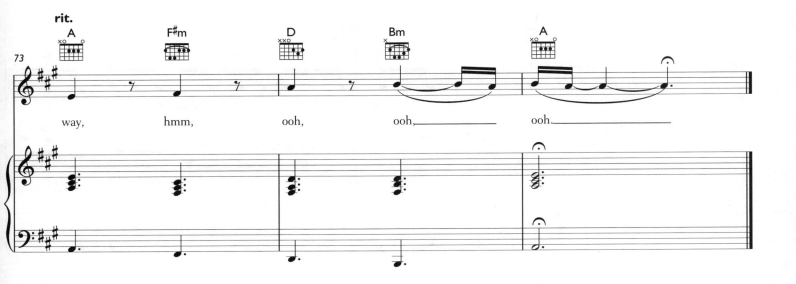

way,        hmm,        ooh,        ooh,_____        ooh_____

# TOO LITTLE TOO LATE

**Words and Music by Billy Steinberg,**
**Josh Alexander and Ruth-Anne Cunningham**

# YOU KNOW I'M NO GOOD

**Words and Music by Amy Winehouse**

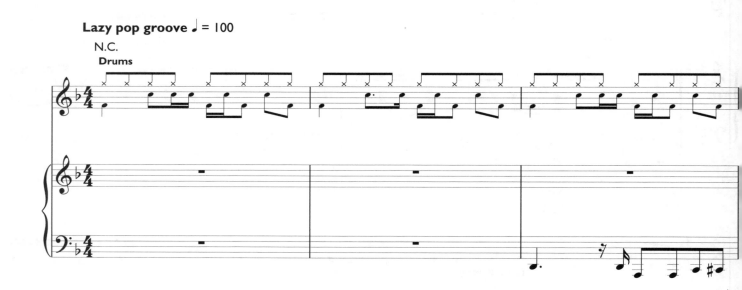

1. Meet you down-stairs___ in the bar___ and hurt,___ your rolled up sleeves___ in your

63

# THINKING ABOUT YOU
### Words and Music by Norah Jones and Ilhan Ersahin

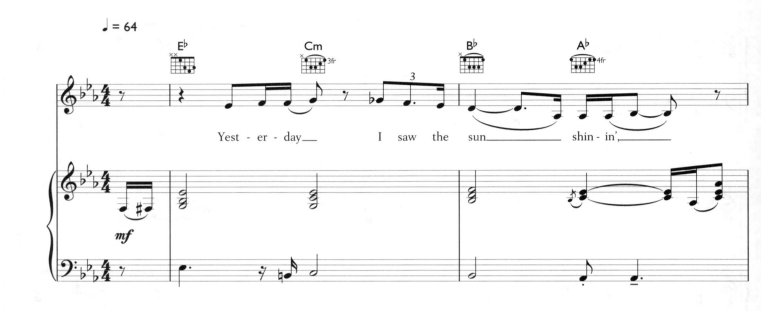

Yest - er - day___ I saw the sun___ shin - in',___

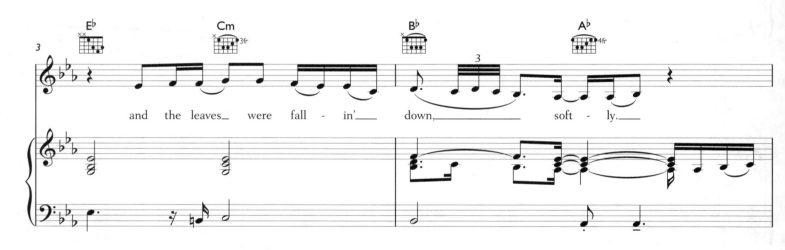

and the leaves___ were fall - in'___ down,_____ soft - ly.___

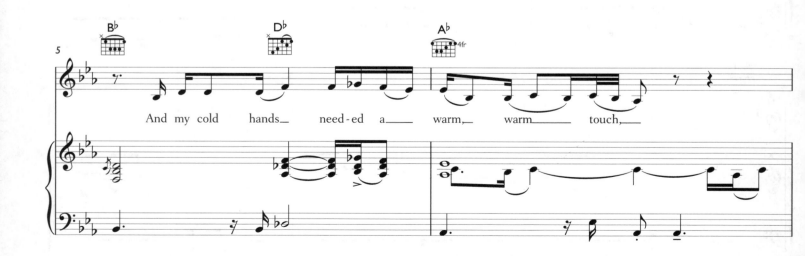

And my cold  hands___  need - ed a___  warm,  warm___  touch,

but I'll be___ think-in' a-bout___ you.___

I'll be think-in'_____ a-bout_____ you._____